THE POCKETBOOK OF PROSPERITY, PEACE & PERSONAL POWER

Karen Cornell, Jane Li Fox &
Marleen Putnam

FIRST EDITION
First Printing, 2006
Cover design by Linnea Armstrong

Library of Congress Control Number:
2006933122
Cornell, Karen, Jane Li Fox & Marleen Putnam—
         The pocketbook of prosperity, peace & personal power/
Karen Cornell, Jane Li Fox & Marleen Putnam 1. ed.
            p.   cm.
            Includes bibliographical references.
            ISBN: 978-0-9797906-0-7
If you wish to contact the authors or would like more information about
this book, please contact the authors in care of Triple Eight Publishing
and we will forward your request.

Karen Cornell, Jane Li Fox & Marleen Putnam
Mountlake Terrace, WA

pocketbook3@gmail.com

Acknowledgement

We would like to thank our friend Shelley Kaehr for her help and encouragement as we were writing this, our first book. Learning the ins and outs of publishing has been a challenge for the three of us. It has been an interesting and rewarding experience for us. We hope you will find the results as rewarding as we did.

—*The Authors*

Contents

FOREWORD

Several years ago I worked in the field of sales and motivational training under the premise that, although the principles were not entirely new, it was always a good idea to take a refresher course from time to time to remind yourself of things you already know.

In *Pocketbook of Prosperity, Peace & Personal Power*, my friends Karen, Jane Li and Marleen have beautifully reminded us of things we all know to do, but too often forget.

I recommend this book for all of us who need to occasionally get back on track and remember that the universe is a place of unlimited possibility.

Shelley Kaehr, Ph.D.
September 2006

PART ONE
PROSPERITY

INTRODUCTION

When we first started talking about the subject of prosperity, we had no idea it would lead to a book. We were meeting to discuss the marketing of the jewelry for Angelwood Creations.

Jane Li started our discussions concerning prosperity and abundance by telling us about her luck with lottery tickets. This got us all thinking about the good and unexpected things that had been happening for each of us. So we decided that each time we met, we would share our stories of prosperity.

The stories began to be really exciting. Karen worked a Halloween Party (doing readings) and received a $100 tip!

Marleen was given a trip to Missouri to see a friend she hadn't seen for many years.

Jane Li went to buy flowers at a nursery. A clerk came up to her and asked her if she had a coupon for the sale occurring that day. When Jane Li said no, the clerk pulled a coupon from her pocket and said, "Here. This is for 20% off on your flowers."

What we began to realize is that as we focused more and more on our prosperity, more and more prosperity showed up! It became clear to us that whatever we concentrated on was what we were manifesting.

And then in a phone message, Jane Li said, "We need to write a book about prosperity." And the rest, as they say, is history.

SO WHAT DO PROSPERITY AND ABUNDANCE MEAN TO YOU?

Most people think of abundance in terms of money and things. But abundance comes in many forms. There are different kinds of wealth, and wealth means different things in different cultures. In some cultures, prosperity is measured in goats!

There was a story in our newspaper about two young boys. One boy, whose family lived on a farm and had very little, thought he was rich because of all the glass jars of preserved food that were lined up on shelves in his cellar. The other boy, whose family lived comfortably, felt he was poor because he didn't have the same expensive game as his best friend. It is all in one's perception. When you feel you are deprived, look around at your surroundings and be grateful for all you see in your world. Gratitude is an essential ingredient in prosperity.

Another form of abundance is health. (Jane Li says you can't go shoppin' if you can't get out of bed!) Before you read any more, stop and take a moment to write down what prosperity and abundance mean to you.

We recommend starting a prosperity journal. As good and prosperous things happen in your life, write them down. On a "bad hair day", you can go back and read your journal and see how prosperous you really are!

Count your blessings!
(Gratitude goes a long way in
creating abundant energy)

TAKE RESPONSIBILITY FOR YOUR ABUNDANCE

So, are you sitting around waiting for your good to fall in your lap? John Randolph Price says, "Don't sit around waiting for your good to fall in your lap. Your lap may be far removed from the point of contact!" The word "can't" needs to be removed from your vocabulary. Robert Kyosaki, in "Rich Dad, Poor Dad" writes, "Instead of saying 'I can't afford it', say 'How can I afford it'?"

Appreciate and recognize your talents and abilities. Don't sell yourself short. Fear, doubt and limitations are all negative emotions that will stop your flow of abundance. Be open to new ideas for creating prosperity and abundance no matter where they come from, (Even when they sound stupid!) Have faith in yourself and in the Universe.

DON'T GIVE UP!
(The pot of gold at the end
of the rainbow really can be
yours!) And don't forget,
take responsibility for your
abundance. (Don't wait for the
other guy to do it for you!)

"STUFFOLOGY" 101

One of the tricks in life is to realize that everything in your life has its time. Things and people come into your life for a reason—and a time. When that thing or that person has done its job, it leaves you. The trick is to let it go!

In our society, people have become huge collectors. We pack away, store, collect and move around tons of "stuff". It truly is exhausting! But more than that, when your life is stuffed with "stuff", there is no room for bringing in new things—or ideas—or abundance.

Abundance does not necessarily mean having your life cluttered up with tons of "stuff". Things weigh you down. They take up space in your physical world and in your mind. So let go of your "stuff."

"Stuff" means clutter, and clutter means junk, and junk isn't usually worth much! Try recycling your "stuff" to a new and grateful owner. Make room in your mind and in your heart and in your space to bring in new ideas and abundance.

*Is there a dumpster
in your future?*

Misery Loves Company

There is always someone who wants to bring you down. If you have a creative idea, they will put it down.

In the Garden of Life, we cross paths with many people. Some will be roses and some will be weeds. Cultivate the roses. They will always be a positive and uplifting influence in your life. Pull the weeds. They are a negative influence and will choke the life and creativity right out of you!

Think of yourself as a two-way radio with an antenna that you can raise to receive a radio frequency. That antenna opens you to any kind of energy signal. When negative energy comes in through the antenna, what do you get? STATIC! When you fine- tune the station, you then get a clear signal. Being around negative people, or in negative situations, brings "static" into your life and experience.

So how do you recognize a negative person? Let us count the ways.

They are often judgmental, angry, fearful, doubtful, confused, dishonest, and suffering from low self-esteem and a sense of self-worth that is somewhere below the basement level. They may exhibit all of these characteristics or only a few. They live in a world of perpetual "victim-hood". Their radio is a few circuits short of a good connection!

The effect on you, as a person, can be devastating. You will find yourself being exhausted. Worse yet, if there is prolonged contact with a negative person, or a negative situation, you can become quite ill. Remember that the body reflects whatever is going on with the mental, spiritual and emotional parts of you. And you need to be on guard that you don't pick up these negative habits yourself. It is often easier to be negative than positive.

Be aware of your surroundings and don't be afraid to weed your garden!

It is not your job to save the other person. That is their responsibility. (But you might suggest they tune into a station with a higher frequency!)

The Appreciation And Gratitude Theory

The first thing that comes to mind about appreciation and gratitude is that we are just fortunate to be here, suckin' air on planet Earth! All too often, we get hung up on material possessions. We just know we won't live if we don't get that new barbeque, or that big TV, or that Gucci bag. We drive around in our big SUV's, barely even noticing the trees or the mountains or the water, hurrying to the next appointment, dashing in to grab some food and then watch TV. Then we go to bed and start it all over the next day.

We pay no attention to the little things in life. What about the people who cannot see to read a book or watch a sunset? What about those who cannot hear the birds that sing, or who cannot walk along a woodsy path?

What about those who cannot smell the flowers or taste the fine flavors of good food? We take it all for granted as we rush around not paying attention to these things, which if taken away (any or all), would drastically change our lives.

It is time for each of us to stop and be grateful for our health, for our loving relationships, our children, our freedom, our ability to use free will and free choice, and for all the opportunities we receive.

Are you a "poor me-er"? Do you think the world owes you something? Do you live by Murphy's Law?

Get a grip! It's time for you to understand that the Universe is like a big mirror. The images (or energy) that you project will be reflected right back atcha'! In other words, you are going to get from life exactly what you put into life.

For example: If you want more love in your life, be a loving person. If you want more money in your life, be a generous person. These are not new concepts. These are old concepts, tried and true.

So be grateful for who you are. Be grateful for what you have. Don't be afraid to say "thanks" to the Universe once in a while!

Developing an "attitude of gratitude" will go a long way toward bringing you the important things in life. (Go on a "rampage of appreciation!")

THE ART OF LIMITLESS THINKING

When was the last time you "thought" about what you are "thinking" about? Thoughts are like things. They are an actual energy—you just can't see them. Every thought and idea goes out into the Universe and collects like energy and then comes back to you. Sort of like a boomerang. So, be aware of what you are thinking or saying or doing, or you are apt to get hit in the head with that boomerang!

There is a tendency in our society today to put limitations on ourselves and others. Do you see your life as going nowhere or do you see that the "sky is the limit"?

Who have you been blaming for the way your life has been going? God? The devil? Your Mom? Your Dad? Your mate? How about looking in the mirror and considering the thought that you may be responsible for the events that take place in your life?

Your thoughts, words and actions create the events in your life. If you don't like the way things are going, change the way you think, speak and act. Take responsibility for the direction of your life.

You must first identify what you want from life. Make a list. The Universe will bring what you ask for, but if you put out "fuzzy" you will get back "fuzzy." So be specific. And be positive! Know that this is already done and that what you desire, "desires" you. Word your requests in the present tense and positively.

Appreciate and recognize your talents and abilities. Believe in yourself. (Don't sell yourself short.) Who knows, you may be able to throw away your Prozac!

Be open to all new ideas, no matter where they come from. Ideas may come from unlikely places or people. Listen! You have the ability to create whatever you want.

Dare to take a risk. Go for it!
Remember, the Universe is there
to be your parachute.

ABRACADABRA, ALAKAZAAM!

Is your magic Genie stuck in a bottle? We all have a magic Genie, you know. It comes in the form of an angel.

There are legions and legions of Guardian Angels. Plenty to go around. Everyone has at least one. Getting your angel out of the bottle is easy. Just start talking to him. Don't be afraid to try it. They really have quite a wonderful sense of humor.

Angels are with us to help us and pave the way for all magical experiences that our hearts' desire. Nothing is impossible with an angel. They are often responsible for those unexplainable coincidences that happen to you frequently.

Most of us are yearning to have a little magic in our lives. It is one reason the *Harry Potter* books and movies are so popular. If we could only believe that life is magic, and that we have the magic of the angels at our disposal 24/7, life would be so much better.

So, what do you say to your angel? One of Karen's favorite lines is, "Hey guys, you on vacation or what?" Marleen's is, "Yoo hoo, I need an answer here." Jane Li hollers, "Tech support! Get with the program down here!" The point is, you don't have to have a formal prayer, or a prayer book, to connect with your angels. Say what you need to say. They are standing right beside you.

Of course, sometimes it may be necessary to call in the big guns. If you are not familiar with the Archangels, let us introduce you to a few of them. Each has a special assignment. Archangel Michael: protection. Archangel Raphael: healing. Archangel Gabriel: communication. Archangel Jophiel: Creativity and beauty. Archangel Chamuel: relationships. Archangel Zadkiel: Gratitude and forgiveness. Archangel Uriel: peace, harmony and balance.

These are just a few of their abilities. Each Archangel is multitalented and can help you in many ways. Archangels can be in more than one place at a time, so feel free to call on them whenever you need them. They will be there instantly.

All of the Archangels will assist you with abundance. Of course, when you read the above list, all of those things do represent abundance and prosperity. Angels are not serious. They like to have fun. And they like it when you have fun. There is a line that says, "Angels can fly because they take themselves lightly". So, take yourself lightly! Use your sense of humor. Fear stops abundance. Your sense of humor keeps fear at bay.

*So, ask, ask, ask and
laugh, laugh, laugh.
Soon you will be laughing
all the way to the bank!*

MAKE IT HAPPEN

Making it happen is called *manifesting*. And manifesting starts with an idea.

Idea is another word for *imagination*. Your imagination knows no limits. Anything you imagine is possible if you are willing to think "outside the box".

Once your imagination sprouts an idea of what you want, say it out loud. This signals the Universe that you "intend" for it to happen. This is called "setting an intention". Now you have thought it—and spoken it—and it is time to do something!! (This may include getting up off the couch and turning off the television set!)

You can program what you desire by making a very specific list that describes all of the details of whatever it is you want.

Let's use buying a new car as an example. Write it down. Write down the make, model, color, type of transmission, type of interior, all accessories, everything you want. (Karen once did this and got everything she asked for. But— she forgot to put in electric windows. Rolled those windows up and down for 8 years!)

And, it is not enough to say, "I would like to see a new car in the driveway." The next thing you see may be a new car in the neighbor's driveway!

So be specific. Have fun with it! Create some excitement! If you want a new car, go test drive the car of your dreams. If you want a new house, go to open houses on weekends. Your own enthusiasm and emotion creates an energy that goes out into the Universe and searches for your desire. The Universe then starts bringing you opportunities.

Now it is your turn. As opportunities arise, follow through with action. Don't sit around and wait for someone else to do it for you. You need to network. Talk to people. Share your dream. You never know who knows somebody—that knows somebody—that knows somebody else—that has exactly what you want. It is called synchronicity.

We would like to point out, as we have previously, that there are always people who will throw cold water on a hot idea. So it might be wise to be careful who you talk to if you know you have a very negative friend or relative.

That advice applies to you as well. You came up with a good idea. You created an intention. Don't shoot yourself in the foot by finding a dozen reasons why your idea won't work.

Finally, we would like to say that in our Universe, all things are in Divine Order. Things may not always come to you as you thought they would, but will always come to you as they should. Your dreams and desires will always be brought to you in the best way possible—often in a much better way than you could have imagined. And by the way, it never hurts to say a little prayer, and then "Let go and let God".

We would like to leave you with this final thought on prosperity:

Follow your dreams. Dreams can become reality in the blink of an eye!

THE ULTIMATE FORMULA FOR BEING ABUNDANT (HELP, GOD! I'M SICK OF BEING POOR! GET ME OUT OF THIS MESS!)

- *Diversification.* This is but one idea in the making of abundance. (Don't get stuck in a rut. Ruts are usually muddy!)
- *Appreciate and recognize* your talents and abilities. (Don't sell yourself short.)
- *Be open to all new ideas* for making money, no matter where they come from. (Even when they sound stupid.)
- *Use your imagination.* (Creativity is often the mother of invention.)
- *Dare to take a risk—Go for it!* (Remember the Universe is there to be your parachute!)
- *Do the things you love the most.* (Who wants to be miserable in their work every day?)
- *Follow your dreams.* (Dreams can become reality in the blink of an eye!)
- *Count your blessings.* (Gratitude goes a long way in creating abundant energy.)
- *Take responsibility for your abundance.* (Don't wait for the other guy to do it for you.)

- *Don't give up!* (That pot of gold at the end of the rainbow really can be yours.)
- *Use your sense of humor.* (Fear stops abundance. Your sense of humor helps keep fear at bay. Keep laughing and soon you will be laughing all the way to the bank!)

PART TWO
PEACE

INTRODUCTION

When was the last time you awoke in the morning and felt a real sense of peace about the coming day? When you get out of bed, are you groaning and moaning about life? Do you say "Good morning God" or "Good God, it's morning!"? If you are worrying about everything in your life, perhaps "peace" is the missing piece!

Most of us hit the floor running each morning. Our minds are racing, our thoughts are fragmented and of course just as you are ready to run out the door, the cat coughs up a fur ball in the middle of your bed and the toilet overflows!

Since we are "energy beings," the energy we create, creates what is going on around us. Crazy, confused energy creates crazy, confused situations. So with your scattered energy, you have set the tone for your day. We guarantee that by the end of your day, you are going to be up to your neck in quicksand. And probably wondering why.

Read on, dear readers. The purpose of this section of our little book is to help you avoid the quicksand altogether.

The "Tudes"—Quietude and Solitude

We can already hear you screaming: "Quietude and solitude—are you nuts? I've got kids, a spouse, a job, a house and a yard to take care of. When do I have time for quietude and solitude?"

We understand your dilemma. All three of us have been there. We have all raised kids (Karen has six!). Two of us were single mothers. We all worked outside the home. For all three of us, our specialty was keeping everyone else happy, with little regard for ourselves. Sound familiar?

Here's what we found out (the hard way). If you don't take care of yourself first, you're not going to be worth beans at taking care of anyone else! It is really important, when your life is stressful, that you find a way to carve out some quiet time for yourself—even if it is only a few minutes each day.

Maybe it is your first cup of coffee before everyone gets up in the morning. Maybe it is a few minutes for meditation after everyone else is in bed. Or perhaps it is walking your dog after dinner. (Pets are great stress reducers.) It's up to you to find the time in your schedule for that little bit of solitude. Don't wait for it to happen. Make it happen!

We love the idea of having a meditation room, or taking a yoga class three times a week. But for most of us, that is often unrealistic. So think in terms of the "little moments" when you can be quiet, alone and just catch your breath. Use your alone time to regroup, recharge and relax.

The less time you spend being in a cyclone, the more peace you will find in your life.

WHAT IS TRUE HAPPINESS FOR YOU?

True happiness for each person is different. It is important to recognize that what makes you happy today may not be what made you happy five years ago. And, five years from now, happiness may come in a different form.

The people who seem to be the happiest, are the ones who seem to live in the "now." They don't need "things" to be happy, but are just enjoying each moment of their lives.

As we have already mentioned, we must slow down and quiet down to recognize the things that create real happiness in our lives. How long has it been since you consciously appreciated your surroundings and the people in your life? Or even really smiled at yourself in the mirror?

All too often, we think that the amassing of "things" will make us happy. And then we complain when we have to take care of these "things." True happiness most often involves simplicity. The beautiful sunset; the sound of the ocean waves; the perfect rose in the garden; the smile from someone we barely know — these are all the simple things in life that cannot be bought. It's all been said before, but we are saying it again. The best things in life are free!

So what do you have in your life that makes you happy? Your children? A special relationship? Your job? Your hobby? Your home? Imagine what your life would be like if any one of those things were not there. Most of us tend to focus on the future, rather than realizing that what really matters to us is already present in our lives. Consequently, our lives are full of regrets instead of appreciation.

Have you ever attended the funeral of someone you cared about, and regretted that you had not spent more time with that person? Or had not said "I love you" and now it's too late? Almost all of us have had these experiences. The only thing you have is this moment. Use each moment wisely to nurture appreciation rather than regret! You cannot change the past and the future is unknown until you get there. So stop and smell the roses NOW!

Just like the measles,
happiness is contagious.
You just don't get the rash!

Sharing Your Happiness

Now that we have you focusing on happiness, let's talk about sharing it with others.

You have no idea the effect you have on others as you go through your daily routine. A smile, as you pass someone you don't know, may be the only smile they will see all day.

When you share a fleeting moment, such as a smile, you are sharing energy.

If you are giving off negative energy, such as a frown, you are bringing the other person down.

When you share your positive energy, you become the uplifting person. Positive energy begets positive energy.

We aren't going to beat this subject to death. We are just asking you to share a smile—share a hug—share your own happiness.

Share your happiness,
it's good for ya'!
(and the other guy too!)

BETTER UNDERSTANDING OF EARTH
AND ITS CREATURES

All living things, ourselves included, thrive best in peaceful conditions.

There is a big difference between "surviving" and "thriving." A person who is in "survival" mode is struggling, and struggle can involve many different things. It can mean not enough food, no home, no job, difficult relationships, and no hope for life improvement. Their lives are often filled with inner turmoil. They feel abandoned and unloved, as if no one cares. They are "living," but not "thriving."

When you are "thriving," you see life as an endless path of opportunity. You have hope and look forward to each day with anticipation and enthusiasm. You have an overall sense of well-being and an inner knowing that life is good!

"Thriving" means having the ability to create life as you want it to be. It is knowing that whatever your needs are, they will be met. You have the knowledge that you are supported from without and from within.

Most people think that their life will get better only when outer circumstances change and improve. (i.e. a new car, a better job, a bigger house, more money, a better relationship), when in reality nothing changes until you realize you are the one making the choices and writing the script!

It is important here to understand the results of negative and positive thinking. The more anger and negativity you have, the more you struggle. Hate and war are negative and destructive energies. Love and peace are nurturing energies. On a global scale, look at the lack of vegetation, greenness and resources in places where war is a daily occurrence. Where there has been negative energy for a long period of time, we see barrenness and starvation. With love, caring, nurturing and understanding of ourselves and one another, everything on the planet thrives.

Each of us can contribute to a thriving planet by coming to terms with the idea that our thoughts and actions do make a difference. Make up your mind now to be a positive and peaceful force in your own part of the world.

Are you a rose or a thorn?
The choice is yours!

DOOMSDAY PEOPLE

In the Pocketbook of Prosperity we talked about negative people and their influence on those around them. We bring this subject up again because if you are wanting peace in your life, you must have the support of positive people. These are people who care about your ideas, listen to what you have to say and encourage you.

"Doomsday People" — and they come in many forms (mother, father, sister, brother, best friend etc.) — won't hesitate to assure you that your ideas are really stupid! Have you had that experience? You are really excited about a venture, only to have someone rain on your parade.

Sometimes we expect our family members to be supportive of our ideas, when nothing could be further from the truth. It is often those closest to us who "pooh-pooh" our ideas the most. The best we can suggest here is that you thank them for their input, and then quietly move on and proceed with your own plans. Do not discuss your ideas with them any further.

You are the one who will make things happen. Believe in yourself. As you do, you will attract support from the most unexpected people and places. Peace always comes to those who believe in themselves.

A hug a day keeps the curmudgeons away!

Turning Fear Into Courage

There is more than one kind of fear. We have unfounded fears that have no basis in reality. We also have the in-built type of fear that says, "I am in physical danger."

Knowing the difference between these two is of paramount importance. Built-in fear that protects you is always to be followed. You don't want to step in front of a truck or stand outside in a lightning storm. Pay attention to your intuition. It will always keep you safe.

We wish to address the "unfounded fears." These are the ones that keep you from moving forward to achieve peace in your life. What are "unfounded fears"? These are: the fear of taking a risk, fear of rejection, fear of abandonment, fear of failure, fear of success, fear of appearing stupid, fear of displeasing those closest to us, fear of losing money and material possessions and the biggest one of all — the fear of change!

There is not one of us who has not experienced at least a couple, if not all, of these fears. Now how can you be peaceful if you are afraid all the time? Fear is a major detour from "peaceful".

The word FEAR is an acronym for FALSE EVIDENCE APPEARING REAL. This means we believe there is a truth in our situation that doesn't really exist. Situations that cause us to "fear" include not being informed, being afraid of the unknown, illness, the media, our pro-gramming from childhood (i.e. religion, parents, schools, negative childhood experiences), and fatigue. (Vince Lombardi said "Fatigue makes cowards of us all.")

All these things tend to surface at 3:00 a.m. We call them "the 3:00 a.m. willies"! You know what we are talking about. You wake up, go to the bathroom, get back in bed and BAM! Out goes the light, on goes the mental tape and for the rest of the night you are quaking in your bed thinking about everything that has happened, could happen, might happen, will happen and never will happen, but you think about it any-way!

So, how do you push the "stop" button? We suggest a mantra that works for Marleen. Close your eyes and say quietly, "peace be still" sev-eral times until you feel a peacefulness coming over you. Your mind will quiet very quickly and allow sleep to come. Jane Li turns on the light, makes a list of everything she is worrying about, and then writes down the possible solution. Turn those over to your guides and angels and go back to sleep. Karen tends to bypass the list (too much work) and just hollers at the angels for help!

In your waking moments, when everything seems to be falling apart and fear grabs you, we would like to share with you an idea from Mary Crowley, a wonderful friend and boss both Karen and Marleen worked for in the 1970s.

Mary said, "If you really must worry, set a time for it. Get yourself a comfortable chair and go sit in a room from two to three o'clock on a Thursday afternoon. Worry your little heart out and then be done with it. Get up and get going. You are done for the week!"

Mary also said, "Worry is a misuse of the imagination. Ninety-five percent of what we worry about never happens and the other five percent we can't do anything about anyway, so why are we worrying?"

Fear is an illusion, dear ones. Peace and happiness are the real feelings we were meant to have.

To gain courage, you don't have to follow the yellow brick road. You can find your own courage within.

PATHWAY TO PEACE:
ACCEPTANCE OF ONE ANOTHER

If you are ever going to have peace in your life, it is necessary to have relationships with people that are non-judgmental and accepting of one another. This may sound easy, but it can be very challenging.

First of all, how you react to others is very dependent on how you feel about yourself. What do you say to yourself when you look in the mirror? Do you see the "pimples" or the "dimples"? If you are seeing yourself in a negative way, you are most likely seeing those around you in a negative way as well.

Dear friends, this is not the pathway to peace. So the first step is to love yourself and the next step is to consciously practice being non-judgmental of yourself and others. Every person has their own path to walk, which may look very different from yours. There is an old Indian saying that says, "Do not judge me till you have walked a mile in my moccasins."

This brings us to the subject of "labeling." We live in a society that tends to put labels on people. Most people are inherently good people.

But we have all learned patterns of behavior that make us look and feel less than lovely.

You may put a label on someone based on how they dress, where they live, how much money they make or how much education they have. But this is almost assuredly not who they are. If you can learn to see beyond the "false exterior" and accept the fact that each person is basically good, your relationships will be much more rewarding and peaceful. Even your so-called enemies may become your friends!

One step beyond being non-judgmental is learning to "value" each person for who they are. There is something to be learned from everyone who comes in to your life. We don't always see it at the time. It may be days, months or even years before we realize what we learned in that relationship, or before we can even put a value on it. But rest assured, at some point, you will realize what that person brought to your life and you will be able to appreciate it.

It is necessary to acknowledge that we don't always see the "bigger picture" and to accept that "all things are always in Divine Order."

The level of peace and love in your life will only be as high as the level of your consciousness.

PROMISE YOURSELF...

...To be so strong that nothing can disturb your peace of mind.

...To talk health, happiness and prosperity to every person you meet.

...To make all your friends feel that there is something in them.

...To look at the sunny side of everything and make your optimism come true.

...To think only of the best, to work only for the best and expect only the best.

...To be as enthusiastic about the success of others as you are about your own.

...To forget the mistakes of the past and press on to the greater achievements of the future.

...To wear a cheerful countenance at all times and give every living creature you meet a smile.

...To give so much time to the improvement of yourself that you have no time to criticize others.

...To be too large for worry, too noble for anger, too strong for fear and too happy to permit the presence of trouble.

— Author Unknown

PART THREE
PERSONAL POWER

INTRODUCTION

Twenty-five years ago, Shirley MacLaine began talking about "Creating Your Own Reality" and everyone went "Huh — what is she talking about?"

In this part of our book, we would like to show you what this concept means and how easy it is to accomplish getting what you really want.

Most people have no idea that what is happening to them today is the result of a thought or an action that they had previously.

It is so much easier to blame everything happening in your life on someone else.

Does this sound familiar to you? Read on, dear reader. We have news for you!

The Blame Game vs.
Creating Your Own Reality

What does it mean to "create your own reality"? It means to create (for yourself only) life as you want to experience it. (Warning: Life as you wish to experience it may not be right for someone else, no matter how close they are to you.)

How do you create your own reality? You do it with your thoughts, words and actions. All thoughts, words and actions have either a negative energy or a positive energy. There is no in-between on this idea. Be aware that negative energy is very powerful. All societies today tend much more toward negative thinking than positive thinking. Most people find it much easier to be negative than positive. It is a lot more work to be positive and most people don't want to work at it. Why is that?

Let's start with programming as a child. We have parents, schools, churches and friends, all of whom influenced us, thereby setting the pattern for our reactions as adults, to the media, politics, racial bias, material wealth, religion, education and personal rights. It is easier to play the "blame game" than to accept responsibility for our own thoughts, words and actions. When things go sideways in your life, what do you do? Do you blame your parents, your kids, your pastor, your boss or your spouse? Or do you step up to the plate and admit that you yourself actually may have had something to do with it?

Thoughts, words and actions have an energy. It is easy to recognize the energy in words that are spoken. If someone calls you stupid, how do you feel? (negative reaction?) If someone says instead, "I love you", you have a completely different feeling don't you? (positive reaction?)

As the old saying goes, "Actions speak louder than words". If someone cuts you off in traffic, you are most likely going to see that as a negative action, and it is going to make you angry. But if someone extends a courtesy to you on the road, (a positive action?) it will probably make you happy.

It is up to you how you react to every experience in your life. You have a choice. You can react to an action in a negative manner (blaming someone else), which indicates you are not in control. Or, you can "create" a positive response with a smile and a wave. Again, the choice is yours.

We come now to thoughts. No, we didn't forget about them. Most people don't realize that thoughts are like "things". They are an energy all unto themselves. Since you can't "see" thoughts, (like you do an action) and you can't "hear" thoughts (like you do words), it doesn't occur to most of us that thoughts have any effect on us at all. Of course there are times when you can "read" someone's thoughts by the expression on their face. All thoughts have a very high energy and will have an effect on you whether you realize it or not. This is the same whether you are thinking them, or someone else is directing their thoughts at you.

If you could see negative thought energy, it would appear as shadows. Positive thought energy would appear as sunlight. Do you want to live in the shadows or do you want to live in the sunlight? Your own "thinking" is going to create shadows or sunlight for you. Unfortunately, most of our planet, at this time, is living in "shadow thinking". You can change not only your own life (reality) with "sunshine" thinking, but you can make a huge difference in those around you and the entire planet.

James Allen said, "You are today where your thoughts have brought you. You will be tomorrow where your thoughts take you." This means, dear ones, that you are taking responsibility for everything that happens in your life. It is not something to be afraid of, it is something to be excited about. Because, you can create your life exactly the way you want it! Hurray! Have a wonderful experience.

What makes happy people
different over those of us
who just "go along"?
They take risks!
They make choices!
They dream. They watch
for coincidences.
Richard Bach,
Running From Safety

One, Two, Three — You're It!

There are definitely steps to creating your own reality (life experiences). We see it as a three-step process.

The first step in creating what you want (not what someone else wants for you), is using your imagination. How many ideas have you come up with in your life that went absolutely nowhere? Not all of your ideas are going to be something you really want to do. The trick is to know when to "do" and when to "discard." Is your idea a "mission possible" or a "mission impossible"?

There is no shame in "discarding" an idea. The choice is yours. Every great experience, invention or Nobel Prize winning formula, started with an idea that came from someone's imagination. If you can "imagine it," you can make it happen, if it is right for you. If it is not an idea that is right for you, no matter how hard you try to make it happen, it just won't!

So, when an idea you had fell apart, what did you do? Did you give up? Or did you get a new "idea"? There are no mistakes here. Only detours!

Don't be afraid to make mistakes. Mistakes are merely learning experiences. Mistakes are not bad things. Once again, we must say that we have been programmed by our childhood teachings to think that errors are sinful. Remember, "to err is human, to forgive is Divine." So forgive yourself for what appear to be stupid mistakes, learn from them and move on!

The second step is to take your idea from "imagination" to "visualization" — the drawing board. This process is not the same for everyone. For some, it is as easy as just picturing it in their mind. Others may need to write it down. Still others may need to draw a picture. How you do this is not important. The important part is that you take this step in creating what you want.

Which kind of "creator" are you? (and this is creation). Are you willing to take the risk of putting your ideas on paper? Or do you leave your ideas roaming around out there in the ether for someone else to pick up and act upon? It happens every day. Again, the choice is yours. Once you can visualize how your idea can manifest into reality, you are ready for the next step.

The third step in manifesting is "realization". How do you take an idea from visualization to "making it happen"? Here's where it gets a little tricky. This may require some bravery on your part, because it involves risk. You may have friends or family telling you your idea is not possible. You may fear losing some money — yours or someone else's. But the one that stops us the most often is the fear of failure. (Remember though, we already said, "A failure is merely a lesson learned, taking us closer to the possibility of success.")

For instance, for the three of us, writing this book is a perfect example of what we are trying to tell you in this chapter. We had an idea (imagination). We sat down and made an outline (visualization). And if you are reading it, we made it happen (realization)! And making it happen has really been fun.

In your hand will be placed the exact result of your thoughts. You will receive that which you earn—no more—no less.

—James Allen

Laughter, Confidence and Letting Go

You may wonder why we combined these three thoughts in one title. It has been our experience that confident, successful people laugh a lot more and know how to "let go and let God."

How many times have you said, or heard someone else say, "In ten years we will laugh about this"? Our question to you is, if you can laugh about a situation in ten years, why wait? Laugh about it now!

Laughter is the best medicine for any problem. When you laugh, you are shifting your attention away from the problem. It relaxes you and changes your attitude about what is happening.

If laughing doesn't seem plausible at the moment, take a break. Go see a funny movie, watch a funny television show, read a funny book. While you are laughing, this is distracting you and helping you to re-focus. Laughter can actually make you feel better physically. There is a book out about a doctor who says he cured himself of cancer with laughter. If this sounds unbelievable to you, just watch how you feel after laughing at something really funny. Don't you feel lighter in spirit? More positive in attitude? Isn't it true that some of your strongest memories are of happy times that made you laugh? Some of the best movies and television shows have been the ones where the people are living experiences exactly like the ones you and I live every day. But, they make it funny. And they make us laugh in the process. And more, they show us how to bring that feeling into our own lives. They show us, (and this is all important) how to laugh at ourselves. Don't take yourself and your life situations so seriously. Don't laugh a little. Laugh a lot!

Confident people know how to laugh at themselves. They are not afraid to show themselves as vulnerable because they have confidence in their ability to find a solution to their problems. Confidence gives us the ability to laugh at ourselves and propels us forward in our quest to find solutions to our everyday trials and tribulations. Laughter bolsters confidence, makes us feel more positive and capable and able to cope with everyday living. Confident people, more often than not, are naturally positive thinkers.

Positive thinking involves the language of "letting go". And that is a language many people are unfamiliar with. "Letting go" involves the realization that the Universe is like a bank full of solutions waiting for you to make a withdrawal. Confident people don't have to control everything. They know when it is time to do "something" and when it is time to do "nothing". They know how to let go and let the Universe take over. And that is called "just sleep on it".

Personal power is not about controlling everything. It is about recognizing that you only can really control your own life with the choices you make and you leave the rest up to the Universe.

Laugh at yourself.
Have confidence in your
abilities. Let go of the need to
control — NOW.
Because NOW is all we have.

Metamorphosis–
Caterpillar to Butterfly

We looked up the word *metamorphosis* in the dictionary, and here is what we found: it means a change in form from one stage to the next, sometimes by magic. It is a transformation and transition and each of us has experienced this, or something like it, at some time in our lives.

If you read the paper or watch the news on television, you can't help but be aware of huge changes that are taking place in our society and on our planet. Changing weather patterns and global warming are in the news every day. Earthquakes are common occurrences in Japan, other parts of Asia and the Middle East. A tsunami wiped out close to 300,000 people in Indonesia. Our own country was attacked and we lost the twin towers in New York and several thousand people. Jobs that seemed secure with ample retirement were suddenly gone. The point here is, what felt secure in your life up till now may not feel that way anymore.

What does this mean for you? You are being required to give up old energy patterns, old belief systems and old ways of doing things that just don't work for you any more. Scary? You bet! We don't like change and we don't like letting go of things that feel familiar, even when they stink! We are like Linus with his smelly little security blanket!

Now we are confronted with the dilemma of making choices. Oh boy! That's even scarier! Most of us dislike making "choices" because they mean "change." It is important that you understand that there are no "wrong" choices. If you can wrap your mind around that idea, it will take away the fear you feel when you have to make a change in your life.

When things are thrown in your pathway that involve choice and change, are you willing to look at this as an opportunity rather than a threat to your security? Now you are confronted with the opportunity to be responsible for yourself and take charge of your life. An example of this would be—if you have ever been fired from a job, you know what we are talking about. All three of us have had this experience, so we know how it feels.

When you are faced with a change, whether it is your idea or not, it may be hard to see the light at the end of the tunnel. The kicker here is to understand that you will create a new reality for yourself and many new ideas will come to you unexpectedly. This is where you have to have faith that the Universe is just full of answers waiting for the questions to be asked. This is where the metamorphosis begins to occur. You get the ideas, you decide which one(s) to try first and you take action. But remember, "if at first you don't succeed, try another idea"! As we have said before, there are no wrong ideas, no wrong choices, no failures. Nothin' is cast in stone here!

We think the reason that we have so much trouble making changes in our lives and letting go of things and situations, is that we become too attached within our "comfort zone" and to our "things". You may have to make a choice to let go of something old in your life, before the "new something" can come along. It is called "creating a gap in the energy," or, "you can't fill a cupboard if it is already full!" Being open to change and being willing to let go of something and create that change on your own is the key to freedom. It is giving up being a caterpillar and becoming a butterfly!

Enjoy everything that happens in your life, but never make your happiness or success dependent on an attachment to any person, place or thing.
—Dr. Wayne Dyer

Finally...

We have come to the end of our little book. But it is really the beginning for each one of us. As we each walk our own path, we will experience peaks and valleys, wonderful times and difficult times. It is up to each one of us how we choose to face the challenges and appreciate the rewards. No one is going to "do it for you." There are no free rides.

Hopefully, we have given you enough tools to work with, to make your journey a peaceful, prosperous and happy one.

We look forward to seeing you along the way!

LIBERATION

Our deepest fear is not that we are inadequate.
Our deepest fear is that we are powerful
    beyond measure.
It is our light, not our darkness,
    that most frightens us.

We ask ourselves,
    "Who am I to be brilliant, gorgeous, talented
    and fabulous?"
Actually, who are you not to be?

You are a child of the Universe.
Your playing small doesn't serve the world.
There is nothing enlightened about shrinking so
    that other people won't feel insecure
    around you.

We were born to manifest the glory of our true
    nature that is within us.
It is not just in some of us.
It is in everyone.

And as we let our own light shine,
    we unconsciously give other people
    permission to be the same.
As we are liberated from our fears,
    our presence automatically liberates others.

1994 inaugural speech of Nelson Mandela

Printed in the United States
96880LV00001B/166-255/A